BUGGY'S WORLD
Therapeutic Coloring Book

KAILEAH NELSON

Kaileah Nelson

ISBN: 1975962133
ISBN-13: 978-1975962135

For you Buggy,
Here
Is
Your
World.

Kaileah Nelson

Bug

Bug

The
MUSICAL
MOSQUITOS

Kaileah Nelson

The Mosquito Band

Kaileah Nelson

Dancing with Lady Ballerinas

Kaileah Nelson

DJ Scorpion

Kaileah Nelson

The Musical Caverns

Kaileah Nelson

Dancing in the Rain

Kaileah Nelson

Jumping Spider Trampoline

Kaileah Nelson

Bumble Bee's Flower Garden

Kaileah Nelson

Eating Records

Kaileah Nelson

A Fly's Tale

Kaileah Nelson

Snails of the Pond

Kaileah Nelson

The King's Flight

YODELLAYHEEHOOOO

Kaileah Nelson

The Yodeling Cicadas

Kaileah Nelson

Queen of Music

Kaileah Nelson

Let's fly with the Dragon Bug Sisters

Kaileah Nelson

Let's fly with the Dragon Bug Sisters

Kaileah Nelson

The Orchestra Conductor

Kaileah Nelson

Funky Caterpillar

Kaileah Nelson

Kaileah Nelson

All you need is Music

Kaileah Nelson

All you need is Music

Kaileah Nelson

Hunt of the Katydid

3
2
1

Kaileah Nelson

Dance Competition

HT ONLY
BUGS
BUGABOO STADIUM
Tonight the PIANO BUG
Security
VIP Entrance

Kaileah Nelson

WASP security service

Kaileah Nelson

The Railroad Worm's Hideout

Kaileah Nelson

Ride with the Caddisfly

Ride with the Caddisfly

Kaileah Nelson

The Finale Dance

Kaileah Nelson

The Cricket's Lullaby

Kaileah Nelson

The Cricket's Lullaby

www.ingramcontent.com/pod-product-compliance
Lightning Source LLC
Chambersburg PA
CBHW081249250726
48654CB00012B/1549